"A truly delightful colle(
commentary, that is wis
al and intellectual journ

—**Henry Abramovitch**, Founding President
Institute of Jungian Psychology

"David Rosen embodies a gentle, loving presence to the world, and *Soul to Soul* is a testament to the grace and wisdom I have experienced over the many years of our friendship. Reading the aphorisms in this book is a meditative act, as each one invites the reader to pause and linger with David along the way. As I walk with my friend through the pages of his book, I am reminded of the story of Oz. The maxims in *Soul to Soul* remind us that Oz is within and they instill in the reader the gifts of courage, heart, and intelligence needed for that journey."

—**Robert D. Romanyshyn**, author of *The Soul in Grief: Love, Death and Transformation*

"In the world of 10,000 things and in true Taoist fashion, *Soul to Soul* is a simple and refreshing yet deeply intimate collection of musings gathered thus far along The Way of Dr. Rosen's life. Like petals unfolding, apparent throughout is the shedding of Ego and blossoming of Anima, which allows for the gentle, eternal flow of Sophia's divine voice of Wisdom . . . each anecdote and poem illuminating the collective Path of our times like twinkling stars across the midnight sky, each word spoken in a voice of warmth and integrity from a wise old friend."

—**Leigh Ingram**, trauma counselor

"David Rosen is a wise and patient observer of the place where art weaves a tapestry of mind, soul, and body. In *Soul to Soul*, he opens up his vision to the rest of us, offering a welcome chance to reflect, to notice, and to grow."

—**Thom Lemmons**, author of *Blameless* and *Sunday Clothes*

"If there is one unifying thread running through every page of *Soul to Soul*, it is this: psychiatrist, poet, professor, and comic David H. Rosen is a lover. The author of *The Tao of Jung* and *The Tao of Elvis* loves learning; poetry; the power of healing; creating; cooking; the guiding power of dreams; humor; relationship; and, above all, this wounded healer loves wholeness, which includes the mystery that is life, death, and rebirth. Pick up the thread and find your own way to love now."

—**Robert Epstein**, author of *Contemplating Nature: Pictures, Passages and Haiku*

"In *Soul to Soul* we find the wisdom from Dr. Rosen's training in Jungian Analysis, Western psychiatry, and Eastern spiritual philosophy not just filtered through, but irreversibly, alchemically married to what we would only ignorantly call the 'accidents' of his character. These are not the aphorisms of a misty, intangible Lao Tzu, but those of a blue-eyed, brown-haired, perennially tanned Jewish Buddhist psychiatrist and passionate Elvis fan with multiple sclerosis who played center for objectively the worst team in college basketball history. This is truly from his soul to yours, and through it the reader will feel freer to share their own soul with the world."

—**Nathan Mascaro**, Atlanta VA Trauma Recovery Program and Emory School of Medicine

"The thoughtful result of a wide-ranging creative life—to reflect on, to reread, to rejoice in."

—**Verena Kast**, Professor of Psychology, University Zurich

Soul to Soul

Soul to Soul

—— Aphorisms for Life ——

By David H. Rosen

Foreword by
Annahita Varahrami

RESOURCE *Publications* · Eugene, Oregon

SOUL TO SOUL
Aphorisms for Life

Resource Publications
An Imprint of Wipf and Stock Publishers
199 W. 8th Ave., Suite 3
Eugene, OR 97401

www.wipfandstock.com

PAPERBACK ISBN: 978-1-7252-9573-5
HARDCOVER ISBN: 978-1-7252-9572-8
EBOOK ISBN: 978-1-7252-9574-2

03/12/21

Also by David H. Rosen

Educational & Scholarly

Evolution of the Psyche (with Michael C. Luebert)

Medicine as a Human Experience (with David Reiser)

The Tao of Elvis

The Tao of Jung: The Way of Integrity

*Transforming Depression: Healing the Soul
    Through Creativity*

Patient-Centered Medicine: A Human Experience
    (with Uyen Hoang)

Soul Circles: Mandalas and Meaning
    (with Jeremy Jensen)

*LESBIANISM: A Study of Female Homosexuality With a
    New Father-Daughter Dialogue* (with Rachel Rosen)

Collections of Poems and Haiku

Clouds and More Clouds

Every Day is a Good Day

The Healing Spirit of Haiku (with Joel Weishaus)

In Search of the Hidden Pond

Living with Evergreens

Look Closely

Spelunking through Life

Torii Haiku: Profane to a Sacred Life

"The soul's journey to the Divine. . .
follow the child of true Humanity within."

The Gospel of Mary of Magdala
by Karen L.King

Foreword

Picture this. It's the first day of Honors Psychology & Religion class at Texas A&M University. There are only 30 students in the small high school-like classroom rather than 100-200 students in your typical auditorium classroom. The professor walks in. He has a boom box in his hand (mind you, this is 1998) and places it on his desk. The pre-class chatter slowly dwindles as he pushes play and REM's "Losing my Religion" plays through the speakers. The professor, Dr. David H. Rosen, hasn't said a word yet but starts writing the lyrics of the song on the chalkboard as we listen. Once the song is over, Dr. Rosen's first words to the class are framed as a question—What does this song mean to you?

Over the last 22 years of knowing David Rosen as a professor, mentor, friend, and most recently, Godfather, that first encounter with him in 1998 perfectly encompasses his teaching style, way of being in the world, and deep wisdom. David truly embodies the Taoist principles of simplicity, spontaneity, and humility. He teaches as though he has more to learn. He teaches to incite self examination and self-learning. He teaches to allow his students to discover Truth, not just facts. And if you are lucky enough to have him as a friend and mentor in your life (or to find your way to this book), you have likely heard his wise, simple, and life-changing aphorisms. David did a good job capturing most of the aphorisms he lives by in this book, but he did miss one.

After graduating with a degree in Psychology from Texas A&M University, I moved to Seattle, WA to volunteer with an organization serving homeless youth. During that time, I experienced my first adult heartbreak after having been dumped by my college boyfriend. I'll never forget walking around "The Ave" in the cold, crying on the phone to David and having him as an empathic, silent listening ear on the other end of my 2002 flip phone. After a moment of therapeutic silence, David shared an aphorism (or as I like to call them, David-ism) that has stuck with me ever since. With a break-up, comes a breakthrough. That was not my last heartbreak or break-up. And with each one, I remind myself that something beautiful and growth-producing has the opportunity to break through. And it always does. No matter where you are in your life, career, or journey to self-discovery, may you find one or more aphorisms in this beautiful book to accompany you on your road to soul.

Annahita Varahrami

Preface

Books have always drawn me to them. As a child, I liked to look at the many volumes in our home library. My father had built floor to ceiling bookshelves, and I could get lost in there for hours. Above the library door hung an oval shaped piece from an old stained glass church window, which read "For whatsoever a man soweth, that shall he also reap." As I sat and read through that great diversity of books, I was sowing the seeds for an adventurous writing career, where I have tackled everything from depression and in-depth therapy to poetry, children's books, and cookbooks. The university setting where I have spent many years often forces people to write more narrowly, for very specific and often small audiences. But the word "university" comes from a Latin compound word, *universitas*, that combines *universus* (whole, entire) with *veritas* (truth). So really, if one wants to write about the whole truth, one needs to broaden oneself from academic writing, to writing about and to the uni*verse*. Now, in my sunset years, it occurs to me that all of my own writing has been in tribute to the breadth of the universe of books that awed me in the library during my childhood.

Truth be told, *Soul to Soul* contains philosophical maxims of my life, pearls from my score of books. In keeping with the spirit of diversity, this volume takes bits and pieces from a lifetime of writing. These aphorisms have been important to my life's journey. It is a playful collection that not only saves people from having to read all those damn books, but also draws and weaves together aspects of thought that are otherwise often forced to remain separate—with academic words reserved for certain places, and cookbook jokes for others. I have found the separation model boring, all-too-common, and not very holistic. Admittedly, blurring aphorisms both serious and light-hearted from across different timelines and genres might seem like the eccentric dreams of an old writer who has finally lost his marbles. Fortunately, many people and cultures in the world value the wisdom and play of both children and the elderly. My childhood self saw reading and writing as a nonlinear adventure, and now, returning to that insight as an elderly person, that is the wisdom that I hope to have captured in this book.

Acknowledgments

I thank Annahita for her kind and thoughtful foreword. I want to thank Rebekah Sinclair for her support and help in typing this manuscript. And I want to thank my lovely wife Lanara for her ongoing love and affirmation. Who could forget Willa, our in-house, philosophical dog. Finally, I appreciate Wipf and Stock publishers for their fine work.

The ego, like Ptolemy's earth, is not in the center; the Self is.

Ptolemy, the Greek astronomer, wrongly assumed that the earth was at the center of the universe. Freud made a similarly incorrect claim, when he placed the ego at the center of consciousness. Like Copernicus, who discovered that *the sun* was really at the galaxy's center, Jung transformed Freud's model, placing *the Self* at the center of consciousness. While the Self is an inner wholeness that connects each individual to nature and other people, the ego is an inner voice that is individualistic and insecure. We're taught to think the ego should be at the center, the one with the reigns. But this makes us act out of problematic emotions like desire and fear: it prevents us from achieving security and safety. However, for Jung, the Self is really the entity at the center, linking each of us to the collective and the divine. What the ego really wants, after all, is healing. So while it might feel difficult, even threatening, to make the ego secondary to the Self, only then can we reach wholeness.

Existentially, it doesn't matter.

For me, this saying means that it is important to accept reality. We are teeny dots on the landscape of the universe. Rather than pretending that *the universe* exists *for us* and our benefit—in an egoistic or prideful sense—we need to recognize that *we* are part of *the universe*. It is helpful to create some distance from our ego, and practice the philosophy of loving acceptance and detachment, so that we can keep things in perspective. Even though it is important for all individuals to create and actualize themselves, we ought not get hung up on making our lives or creative products last forever. We need to balance the joy of our own presence in the world with the recognition that we are just a tiny part of the whole. And being a part of a whole does matter. As a Taoist and Jungian, the concept of the opposite holding their tension rings true. So existentially it does matter.

Other people and cultures matter.

Western cultures often look askance at other cultures and accuse them of being too different or even primitive. For example, historically, the West likes to imagine that *its* citizens achieved all the important "firsts"—the first mathematical systems, first languages, first important scientific discoveries, first to write the novel, etc.. Also, the West likes to imagine other countries as less progressive, more patriarchal, and socially backwards. However history outside the West is peppered with firsts, and many by women. For example, while many scholars mis-attribute the first novel to Miguel De Cervantes Saavedra (*Don Quixote* in the seventeenth century), the world's first full length novel, *The Tale of Genji*, was actually written by a Japanese noblewoman, Murasaki Shikibu, in the eleventh century. This underscores why other cultures are so important and why it is important to respect and learn from them.

The feminine matters.

In the West, there is a focus on the masculine. In Jungian psychology, women and men are often encouraged to develop their *animus*, their masculine side. But equally valid is the idea that both men and women also need to develop their *anima*, their feminine sides. This is the part that often gets repressed by both sexes. But only by fully developing the feminine can there be balance. Jung's view of wholeness (and many other versions of wholeness as well) involves a tension of the opposites. To suppress the feminine in oneself or the world is to throw everything off balance. To help develop these repressed parts of ourselves, we need to cultivate openness, sensitivity, and creativity. The tie between the feminine and these important aspects of human life is very ancient, and is found in the many traditions which refer to the earth as our mother. For example, in the book *Soul Circles: Mandalas and meaning*, the circle is the symbol for the feminine, as noted by various cultures. The following poem honors the feminine side of our world and in us all.

Mother Earth

On mother earth
Every breath
Simple and easy

On mother earth
Universal Tree
Upside down roots

On mother earth
Each spring
Pure and flowing

On mother earth
Giant oaks
And their shadows

On mother earth
Ever present sunrays and
Moonbeams

On mother earth
A puppy
Wants to play

MOTHER EARTH

On mother earth
Verdant ferns
Along the path

On mother earth
After rain
Sunbeam appears

On mother earth
Deep cave
Black with light

On mother earth
Every step
Gentle and measured

Heal the soul through creativity.

Creative activities are essential to maintaining mental health. Art has been a crucial part of transforming depression, hurt, and trauma for myself and others. Creativity helps us integrate these broken or hurt parts of ourselves, by redefining what they mean to us, or putting the pieces together in new forms. I've always said that I paint for my inner well-being, and I write for the same reason. Creating leads to healing the soul. Striving to weave creativity into medicine and psychology has been a major part of my life's work, since I have long believed that artistic activities and processes mirror the creativity required to enhance our emotional well-being. It's noteworthy that the Greek word *psyche* means breath or soul, and inspiration is the way we inhale and live fully.

Physician, heal thyself.

As Hippocrates noted, "It is more important to know what sort of person has a disease than to know what sort of disease a person has." Modern medicine often focuses on the disease only, and fails to take a holistic perspective of the person. But, it is critical for physicians and patients to heed this ancient advice, both in healing themselves and others. For everyone has an inner physician—some version of themselves that strives to be a healer. This lesson is quite special to me. For even as a doctor myself, upon discovering that I had multiple sclerosis, I struggled to come to terms with my own diagnosis. My neurologist said, "It's not a death sentence...there are treatments," but that did not diminish the shock, nor have the medications and treatments brought me back to health. However, MS has taught me much, and prompted me to begin thinking holistically: changing my eating habits and lifestyle choices. I have learned to call on creative insights and invite adventures, doing things I have never done. In this way, I heal parts of myself that doctors alone cannot impact. The following poem expresses the need for each of us to bow our heads and endure suffering as a part of life even as we strive to heal ourselves and others.

The Art of Suffering

I bow my head in shame
for all the killings of self and other.

I bow my head in sorrow
for inner and outer wars.

I bow my head in suffering
for all the tragedy that exists.

I bow my head in synchronicity
for we are all the same.

I bow my head in surrender
as it leads to acceptance.

I bow my head in prayer
since it is all we have.

I bow my head in love
as that is all we need.

I bow my head in ecstasy
to balance all the agony.

I bow my head in peace
and everlasting gratitude.

Autobiography is healing.

There is another layer to healing ourselves, more conscious than these, and that is the layer of healing the very stories we tell about ourselves. What is our life story? What has made us who we are and what will remain of us once we are gone? This kind of work—the work of telling and re-telling one's own story—is never finished. And it is only through intensive work at this level, through memoir and autobiography, that we can truly find peace. For example, in my first memoir, *Lost in the Long White Cloud: Finding My Way Home*, I write about how I evolved into a medical doctor and only realized later that it was an unconscious effort to heal myself. When I became conscious of that, I became a psychoanalyst. It was through the writing of this memoir that I was able to fully realize this journey and begin to tell a fuller story.

Illness is a great teacher.

I have learned this the hard way; MS has taught me so much. I find it interesting that people always use the shorthand to refer to multiple sclerosis. So I began to reflect on the abbreviation, MS, and how many other things that could mean. Rather than using the two-letter designation to distance myself from the diagnosis, I dove right in, recognizing all ways this condition has shaped, challenged, and even helped me.

MS as Teacher

My Star

My Soul

My Song

My Sage

My Sloth

My Stress

My Shock

My Sanity

My Sonata

My Savior

My Shrine

My Shrink

My Shroud

My Silence

My Sorrow

My Sunrise

My Shadow

My Setback

My Strength

My Solitude

My Struggle

My Saboteur

My Sacrament

Medicine is a human experience, propelled by science but guided by love.

Most people see medicine as purely scientific, all numbers and diagnoses. But it is also an art, an expression or application of creative skill and imagination. Medicine is about people. Many go into medicine to help others and hope to aid the sick, or because they were ill, or knew someone who was. Though it is propelled by numbers, statistics, knowledge of bodies, etc., medicine is a creative use of skills moved by loving ourselves and others.

Desiderata

Desiderata are needed maxims for practicing the ancient calling. They focus on this loving, artful aspect of medicine. I have used these over the years to remind myself and others in healing professions that medicine is for and about people. 1) Remember that being a doctor is an ethical privilege and responsibility. 2) The only way to revolutionize medicine is if healers remember they are free: free to invent, create, and improve both medicine and themselves. 3) Empathize with your fellow professionals and all those you treat. Never lose the knowledge that you are always both doctor and patient. 4) Remember why you became a doctor; do not lose sight of the reasons you entered medicine. 5) Medical school—as well as all graduate training—does not last forever. Nothing lasts forever. 6) You will make mistakes, and do terrible things, but choose to forgive yourself. 7) Despite our wish for certainty, it is important to accept ambiguity and personal limitations. These can be found in *Medicine as a Human Experience,* and in the revised and expanded version, *Patient-Centered Medicine: A human experience,* which I wrote with a former student, Uyen Hoang.

*Loving ourselves allows us
to love others.*

This is one of the hardest lessons. We are born dependent on people, our parents, and we need their care to survive. But at some point, we need to transition from being parented and loved primarily by them, to being loved and parented by ourselves. Only, after capably loving ourselves, can we stand on firm enough ground to love others well. We see this in the story of Opal Whiteley, a childhood naturalist from Cottage Grove, Oregon, in the early 1900s, which I wrote about in *Opal Whiteley's Beginning*. Like charity begins at home, so does love. Love begets love, so love and heal thyself.

By losing, you often win.
Through failing, you succeed.

I am very fond of Taoism. I have been since I first read the Tao of Pooh and the Te of Piglet. But this lesson really hit home in my college years, when "losing" stopped being metaphorical and became literal. You see, I was on a basketball team in college that set and held the national record for the most consecutive losses for nearly half a century (37, as documented in *Hoops and Hoopla*). I realized that it was being a member of a team, and the camaraderie and friendship I found there, that was vital. You can be in a losing relationship or team and still come out with a positive philosophy and healthy perspective.

sauntering through a forest
finally
a hidden pond

Choose egocide over suicide.

When we face difficult times in our lives, like deaths, trauma, and depression, we avoid thinking about how we got there (which would require healing ourselves), and instead think we can solve this pain through suicide. But instead of killing our *selves*, we need to kill our *egos*. This achieves the ultimate release from spiritual and emotional pain and suffering that we often seek in death, and allows a rebirth into wholeness. Our human life span is like a river, with its stagnant places, calmly flowing stretches, rapids, and dangerous whirlpools. These are naturally occurring periods and times of crisis. Although these crisis points are often stressful and filled with despair, they are also openings for change and growth. Egocide transforms the suicidal impulse into the urge to reach for life, joy, and hope. This is an essential spiritual way to understand transforming pain through centering it and then lovingly detaching from it. This is similar to the Buddhist practice of downplaying and emptying themselves of ego.

A crisis is a form of death and rebirth

It is often noted that the Chinese word for crisis is composed of two characters: danger and opportunity. However the second character is more accurately translated as "critical moment," an intense and heightened breaking point. But change can be an opening and often is a rebirth. All phases of life are characterized by crises of identity. Early life crises are frequently about discovering basic components of who we are and our childlike selves die when we discover more mature, settled versions. Mid life crises are often about one's identity with family and profession. Versions of ourselves who might feel trapped or disappointed can be reborn, finding new meaning in places that once felt confining. Late life crises are mostly about identity in one's community, and finding meaning in life, since many older people feel isolated after retirement, the death of friends and relatives, or other absences from society. In these crises, a version of ourselves dies, as we mourn lost connections. But the possibility for rebirth exists even here, as we become new, creative selves, at peace with the processes of life. These crises are all pivotal moments: though terrifying, they can birth new dimensions of our selves. We are forced to figure our own personal myth, why we are each here, and what will be left after we go. Furthermore, it may be possible that physical death is not the end, but also a crisis from which we can be reborn. How exciting to find out what follows our death.

"It's all good."
No, it's all Tao.

The Tao (the Way) is both fixed and moving at the same time. The Tao governs the individual, just as it does visible and invisible nature (earth and heaven). Above is the ancient Chinese pictograph of the Tao, which is linked to the earth. The upper part signifies going step-by-step, but the line underneath connotes standing still. On the right side is a head with hair above, which is associated with heaven, and interpreted as the beginning or source. The original meaning of the whole pictograph is of the Way, which, though fixed itself, leads from beginning to end and back to the beginning.

Dreams make us who we are.

Dreams provide clues to see the truth about our lives, and often lead us into reflections on our most intimate, and often repressed feelings, thoughts, and memories. Carl Jung's autobiography, *Memories, Dreams, Reflections,* is an example of the value of dreams in self discovery. Dreams help us articulate and experience things that are often unknown, or that we may be unwilling to address in our waking life. In particular, *The Interpretation of Dreams,* Freud realized that these little gems allowed us to understand how to resolve, get relief from, and gain insight into conflicts. For example, I once saw a patient who had difficulty with sexual intimacy. But through a dream, she made a breakthrough that allowed her to recall key events from her childhood, which ultimately enabled her to reconnect to her partner. I take dreams very seriously, and have written down my dreams for nearly 50 years. I find they help me clarify my emotions and even offer guidance. Interestingly, we share the capacity to dream with many other species. So in a way, dreams make us human, even as they also connect us to other animals.

Medicine often treats certain life choices as "illnesses" before it begins to understand them as ways of life.

For example, Freud viewed lesbianism as a mental illness. This was often the case because those people that medicine studied were already 'patients'—they were already considered sick, as was the case with the patients with whom Freud worked. So of course, studying lesbianism under these conditions ends up making lesbianism seem like a sickness. I took a different approach and researched normal, everyday people who considered their ways of life (like lesbianism) to be ordinary and acceptable, rather than pathological. Through listening to people's experiences of their rich lives (rather than assuming illness) we can gain more knowledge about these ways of life. Now, *Understanding Lesbianism,* which I wrote with my youngest daughter, Rachel, emphasizes this view.

Everyday is a good day.

This phrase comes from the Japanese author, Natsume Sōseki. In *Zen and Haiku,* a collection of his poems and letters, Sōseki finishes a playful retelling of a well-known Zen dialogue by using the phrase: "Everyday is a good day." As I have grown to understand Sōseki's writing over the years, I have come to see this as an aphorism of optimism. It reflects a philosophy of valuing days and the time we have to live them. If one has to choose what sort of outlook to have—and I have come to realize that our perspectives are choices—why not choose to believe in the goodness and possibilities of each person and each day. Years after this book was given to me by a Japanese friend and colleague, I found a scroll with this Zen phrase in the back corner of an old shop in Kyoto Japan. The scroll has hung in my home for many years and these words have shaped my view of life.

Dreams lead to discoveries.

Dreams allow us to glimpse something new not only in ourselves, but also in the world. Freud laid the foundation for psychologists and others in the West to take dreams seriously as sources of information and creativity. Of course, most Indigenous peoples have known the importance of dreams and taken them seriously for centuries. In any case, Freud believed that dreams not only show us about ourselves, but also allow our imaginations to flourish unrestricted. This is because dreams give voice to things that are not otherwise acknowledged. In fact, many discoveries have first appeared to people in dreams, the way the Benzene ring was first imagined in a dream by August Kekulé. Elias Howe had the idea for the sewing machine in a dream. People are often quick to dismiss dreams, but they carry insights that ought to be taken seriously. Jung built on Freud's theory to claim that dreams are not just representative of individual experiences, but are linked to a collective human unconscious. He also met with the Indigenous Pueblo leader Chief Mountain Lake and highlighted the value of Native knowledge about dreams.

Life and creativity involve facing death.

In order to live and create, we must confront the death of old issues that have blocked our ability to express ourselves. We naturally do this when we change from childhood to adolescence, adolescence to adulthood, adulthood to old age. But we also must confront these issues before initiating vocational changes, creative projects, etc. In fact, to my mind, these metaphorical deaths are not accidental. Rather, we *only* ever choose paths *because* they force us to confront symbolic death and rebirth. When I was in Switzerland carrying out research for *The Tao of Jung*, I thought I was suffering from a heart attack. A friend and colleague took me to see her doctor, who did an exam and an EKG, and said, "No, you're not having a heart attack." On reflection, what was going on was that something had to die in order for me to write the book I was researching. And once your demons die, you can do anything.

Mandala is wholeness.

The mandala represents a circle and the Taoist concept of light. Traditionally, mandalas are drawn in sand, or on the ground, and often they contain many images and colors which represent a coming together of all factors. In many cultures, once completed, the mandalas are allowed to blow away. Their purpose is to educate, teach impermanence and growth, and then to be released. In this way, mandalas represent wholeness. Recently, one of my analysands, Jeremy Jensen, brought mandalas he had made to his sessions. Everything about them was meaningful: the colors, the images, and the stories. They were so beautiful, intricate, and symbolic and became the basis for analysis, and through them he found wholeness. They also evolved into a book we coauthored titled, *Soul Circles: Mandalas and Meaning.*

Patience is a virtue.

It is better to pause and wait than to demand or pressure. We often think of patience as something we should have with and for others. But patience also has a way of helping individuals. We cannot speed up time or life. We cannot make trains arrive faster, or children learn lessons with haste. Our own impatience does not always impact the world, but it can negatively impact our own experience of the world. We can become bitter if we do not allow the world to happen at its own pace. This is a sentiment that is conveyed in the haiku below, drawn from my book, *White Rose, Red Rose*. The first haiku is from my coauthor, Johnny Baranski, and I respond with a call for patience.

> *a train whistle*
> *fades in the moonlight*
> *mountain snow*
>
> *Sitting in the rain*
> *waiting for the train*
> *to nowhere*

Losing things leads to finding things.

This relates to my own philosophy, which is that research—looking for things—is always me-search—the finding of ourselves. There are many things we lose in life—friendships, objects, chances, and so on. On our journeys we often find things that we were not looking for, even if we never find what we are looking for. The seeds of my being a researcher (and a me-searcher) come from active imagination, like the kind one finds in my book, *Samantha the Sleuth*. In that book, Samantha becomes a detective in order to solve the mystery of her missing socks.

Friendship and guidance can help us overcome prejudice.

None of us are isolated individuals. We are meant to be in relationships. Our prejudices are often rooted in deeply personal anxieties about ourselves, rather than about others. They often come from our parents. We need these other relations in our lives to help us get through these prejudices. For example, when I was a child, I did not understand antisemitism. When a childhood friend was not allowed to play with me after school because I was Jewish, his reasons had to be explained to me. I write about this issue in *Zach's Hard Lesson.* But it was really Dave's hard lesson. When our teacher, Mrs. Hayes, said, "You can be friends at school!" she gave us a space to be friends safely and helped my friend deal with the prejudice of his family. So we often played together at recess and sat together at lunch, and found other ways of remaining close.

Loving gifts can break through conflict.

Behind such a gift is mysterious love that can often be felt in the gift when words cannot be heard. Loving gifts are often risks, especially when they come in the context of conflict and one does not know how the gift will be received. Children often know this lesson intuitively. They bring flowers or licorice or other small sentiments to angry parents in attempts to restore peace in difficult relationships. Dogs, cats, and other animals are also known to do this. My learning of this gift came through an incident with my father, which I later published in a children's book titled, *Henry's Tower.* I had built a tower out of blocks and my father knocked it down. Though this caused some anger between us, I rebuilt the tower and decided to try to repair the relationship by giving him something he liked, in this case, licorice. I also tell this story at the beginning of a healing coloring storybook called, *Time, Love, and Licorice.* This illustrates how we can revise and retell painful stories from our past.

Let us love and embrace differences

It is common to think that sameness is good, rather than difference. But difference and diversity are the key to life. Diversity in genetics is the key to a species success, diversity in cooking is the key to tasty food, and so on. These lessons ought to be taught early, so I came up with an alphabet book, *Kindergarten Symphony*, to help with this. I remember loving alphabet books as a way to master the alphabet. But do we need another? Yes. Because each one, like every person, is different. Here is an anecdote to further underscore the importance of this maxim. In 1956 the school systems in Springfield, Missouri were recently integrated and the teachers had the incredible responsibility to help diverse students actualize themselves and overcome centuries of prejudice. I will always remember my teacher that year, Mrs Murphy, who lived this principle. On the first day of class, she asked each student to say his or her name and what we did during the summer. My friend, Joe Price, who was newly integrated into our previously white-only school, went first. He said, "I sang at home and at church. I like to sing." Mrs. Murphy said, "Wow! You're a singer." And then she hugged him and said, "I love you." Wouldn't you know it, that's what Joe became. A singer. She continued to do this with each student.

Less is more.

We often think that more is more. The more we speak, the more we feel, the more we write, the more we achieve, the better we will feel. But I have found that is not the case. How often does a look convey as much as several paragraph's of explanation? We can feel as deeply from a short story, or small haiku, as a lengthy book or play. I once wrote and a edited a series of Ten-Minute plays, *Less is More*, that convinced me that Shakespeare was right: "Brevity is the soul of wit." One of the plays, "A leap for life" was based on actual research with those who survived jumping off the Golden Gate Bridge. I found that by prioritizing minimalism and letting these stories convey their own meaning, I was able to say very important and emotional things in just a few words.

Psyche refers to the psychological, but also to the social and biological realms.

The psyche, an integrative phenomenon, is not just about the internal mental states of a person. The psyche names all the relations which cohere in an individual, both social and biological. For the psyche, while often thought to be something strictly ephemeral, is profoundly related to our bodies. So once again, to address or heal the psyche means taking a holistic approach. The word psyche means soul. So what we're doing is what Plato recommended, joining psyche with soma, the body. Or, as Freud might say, the mind and the body. This wisdom is explored in the *Evolution of the Psyche*. I have always found that one of the best ways to integrate the soul and the psyche is through poetry, specifically through haiku. Haiku take one into nature and remind us that we are bodies that are integrated. The poem below is from *The Healing Spirit of Haiku*.

Dawn on a spring sea—
then a glittering
from a thousand jumping fish

Nature is sacred

As Spinoza said, nature is One. Nature encompasses all that is, including God. Spinoza integrated these two often divergent themes: spirituality and nature. Spirituality is often thought as something that is made up by humans, while nature is what exists beyond and outside of humans. But Spinoza brought the two together through his ethical philosophy. The following haiku captures this for me.

Wind in the pines
angels whispering

Wild . . .
no further proof
of God

Each person has a link to the divine.

However it is difficult to see divinity in ourselves. Historically, people would project this divine link onto religious and political figures, like clergy or Kings and Queens. Kings and Queens gave us the link between being human and being divine—or at least, they gave us the archetype of someone who was between these two. More recently this has been projected onto superstars and pop stars. For example, when I wrote *The Tao of Elvis,* the following was true: no matter where you went in the world, there were three faces that were immediately recognized: Jesus, Muhammad Ali, and Elvis. But the whole point of my book about Elvis is that the divine is within each individual. Just as Elvis did not feel the divine in himself, but chased it externally, so too we often see divinity, safety, and so on as outside of ourselves. Perhaps Elvis would be alive today had he eventually recognized that what he was chasing was inside all along. That is what we all need to recognize: the divine is within us.

You always feel better when you cook and laugh.

What are the two things that make us feel great? Laughter and darn good food. I think it's important that we put these features together. My cookbook, *The Alchemy of Cooking: Recipes with a Jungian Twist*, has recipes written in a humorous way that I hope also convey the importance of Jungian psychology through familiar and everyday practices like cooking. For Jung, there is a technique for analysis called active imagination. This means coming up with an artistic product, which could be a recipe. Jung even practiced this himself. For example, when I first walked into Jung's retreat tower, Bollingen (which he designed himself), the whole first floor is a kitchen. It is filled with recipes hung on wires which Jung used to refer to when he cooked for himself and guests. Jung thought cooking was healing. At the age of 70, when you can finally realize gifts you've never discovered, I became a comedian—that is, I finally accepted the ability to make people laugh and to laugh with them. Comedy has always been important to me. If you have any interest, a bit of my humor is currently online: just search for Dr. Nada live at the Tiny Tavern.

I'm alive because I'm not dead,
but I'm ready to go to glory.

Being alive is glorious. Seizing the day, and being creative in life, is sustaining. And the reason is that I practice death and rebirth everyday. I know that things are constantly dying and being reborn. Every time one lets go of one thing and accepts another, that is a little death and rebirth: a death of certain possibilities and realities, and the bourgeoning of new possibilities. Our culture tends to feel that death is only bad, it is an end, a final termination, that is something to be avoided at all costs. But death is instead folded into life itself, making life possible. It's no accident that the French call making love *la petite mort*, little death. Death is change, a vast wellspring. That's why, when death comes, I will embrace her.

Never trust a computer that you can't throw out the window.

Other people's knowledge, through the computer, is taking over the world. A day will come when the power goes out. It's important to develop your own, internal wisdom, so that you can never have it thrown away. There is always the temptation to appeal to other authorities, other sources of knowledge, rather than oneself. Everyone has their own aphorisms that they live by, no matter what they have heard or read. It is important to stick to these, and be true to oneself. For example, another aphorism, which I like, came from a friend and I as we were speaking together: there is music you'll never hear unless you play it yourself. This speaks to the value of one's own creativity, formal and informal. Like the Delphic maxim says, "Know thyself."

If you want to be happy,
let a vocation adopt you.

Each person has a propensity for some vocation. There are those who love teaching and writing, those who love organization and clarity, those who love the law, psychology, or social work. There are archetypes of different jobs. But do we choose the vocation or does the vocation choose us? For many people I know, finally entering the job that makes them happy was like coming home. It allowed them to actualize themselves and to see that the kind of person they were had a purpose and a calling that was important for and needed in the world. They found their voice or vocation. We think we're going to be happy if we choose our vocation. But to be really happy, one needs to let the vocation choose them.

People give up on love, but love does not give up on people.

We need to be centered in our hearts and love will find us. Our minds can give us excuses and reasons to break off and give up on love. But love is something that is constant, flowing under and around all things. Love never gives up, but is always constant. It is our job to tap into this flow and stay connected to it. The keys are acceptance and discernment. In order to live, speak, and love wisely, we need to embody our own philosophy and become a real friend of truth. To be discerning means that one does not just know much and know it well, but one knows how and when to best apply this wisdom. Wow. Love starts like charity at home. It sounds simple but it's difficult. One must first love oneself in order to love others.

*Love and accept yourself
and others will follow.*

This answers the problem of "how do I love people I dislike or fear." The key is to love those parts of ourselves that we despise or fear in ourselves and others. By "love these parts" I do not mean that we should condone our base fears. But rather that we should start by calming and caring for those parts of ourselves and helping to ease these fears. If we begin by loving and accepting our shadows and our selves, then we lose our reactionary tendencies to others. We can attend to parts of ourselves that are sensitive or scared, and help calm ourselves and other people. This will help promote peace, even if others do not always agree with us. The key is to love others as one loves oneself.

God doesn't judge us,
we judge ourselves.

God is really about our own acceptance of ourselves and other people. We project it onto some parental figure in the sky. But it's really about ourselves. We judge or accept ourselves, it's not something outside of us. This is something that starts within. It's about our inner process, which involves loving oneself. And when you love yourself, you can love other people. Loving other people brings you to community. Loving community is a step to loving the world.

Loving a child is easy to do, loving one's inner child is hard.

Most people find it easy to love children. But, strangely, people have a very difficult time loving their own inner children. We are willing to forgive children for the silly things they do, but then we look at our inner child and blame them for things—for not being loved by parents, for making mistakes, for doing things for which we would forgive any other kid. It's very important that we begin to extend the care, forgiveness, and gentleness that we would give to any children to our inner children. Jung claimed that this process is related to the divine child archetype.

Loving a dog is loving god. Being loved by a dog is being loved by god.

Aren't we fortunate that, in English, god and dog have a palindromic relationship. These words contain each other, and maybe their meanings do as well. This is an interesting relationship because we often think of god and dog as on opposite sides of the human: i.e. god is above humans, and dogs and beasts are beneath. But we ought not think about humans as above or below anything. Instead, the message in this palindrome could be: "as above, so below," or maybe, there is no above or below. There just is and when we find our dog loving us completely, think of God doing the same.

*Ask yourself what would happen
if you said and did nothing.*

We often think of ourselves as lovable based on what we do and how we act. This message is often told to us by our education system, our society, and sometimes, unfortunately, even our parents and relatives. People begin asking "what do you want to do when you grow up," when kids are little. But nobody asks, what kind of person do you want to be? And it's even harder for people to believe that they are going to be loved and accepted just for existing. We need to become individuals who are okay with just being, and who love others just for being. We're not human doings; we're human *beings*.

Modesty is healthy.
Excess is illness.

I know this to be true because I tended to do too much and I became ill. We often are taught that unless we are giving 100%, fully and completely the best at something, then we are no good at all. One person wins the race and everyone else loses. But this kind of thinking can often be about exalting excess, and about letting other areas of our life suffer to succeed and become the best at one thing. For example, at college, students are expected to specialize in one thing—economics, english, psychology, and so. It is good to be specialized, but this kind of specialization can also lead to competition and egoism, and prevent people from becoming well rounded and their true selves. It can also lead to excess, and then reaching fulfillment requires the hard work of ego-cide, or shrinking oneself back to a healthy size.

Aphorisms are like haiku,
they are healing moments.

When you perceive beauty, or truth, you are in a loving relationship with something or someone. You don't have to say anything. Its like being with a rose bush. You don't need to say to the rose bush, "Wow, your roses are very beautiful." You just accept them and interact with them. The same thing is true when you walk in a forest. You just accept the forest, and are rendered speechless. The realization that momentous experience is all you need is something that is captured in both haiku and aphorisms. Aphorisms represent a deep truth: that momentous experience, closeness to wisdom, is all you need. Here is an example of haiku that, for me, capture this fundamental truth.

Finally
looking at a peony
speechless

Wild
no further proof
of God.

In wildness
the cougar on the hill
you can see God.

Parents teach us about
life and death.

We're born from our mother, nurtured by both parents, and they help us to experience and prepare for both life and death. My father didn't quite understand my global aspirations, but my mother was more expansive and helped me embrace both the local and the world. The following two haiku are about losing my parents.

> All leaves
> fall
> day my father died.

> Mother dying . . .
> full moon over
> Kansas City, the world.

Parents are wonderful,
but also grand.

Children are our teachers to be good parents and grand-parents. If you don't get it when you are a parent, you get it when you're a grandparent. Without the daily responsi-bilities, which contained so much of the frustration, all you have are wonderful, idyllic moments. Perhaps that's why they call it "grand" parenting. Because it's all the grandness of parenting and of children, without as much of the chal-lenge. I was very spoiled by my grandparents, as so many grandchildren are. But that makes the relationship very spe-cial. I was so close to mine that, for my first of year college, I chose a school near them so that I could be closer to them.

Nature provides the opportunity for experiencing life and death repeatedly.

In nature, death and rebirth is a common theme. And we often have little deaths in our own experiences—little moments of emptiness, loss, and so on. But there is always a balance.

Late in our lives, my wife and I chose to move to the outskirts of town, into the foothills, where we can witness the cycles of life and also feel our own part in this cycle more keenly. For me, it was hard to leave full-time academia, but that too is just part of my journey, my own cycle of life. Now, the company I keep are bears, foxes, deer, cougars, hawks, vultures, and rabbits. The following haiku were written once we moved to the country, and are from my book, *Clouds and More Clouds*:

Leaving academia . . .
I joined my friends
birds, trees, and wind

My life
a long, slow rain
earth

Alone
until you returned
red dragonfly

The spider web
mysterious spiral
life and death

*Spelunking through life relates
to our struggles and leads
to childlike questions.*

On our journeys of individuation, we repeatedly return to childlike questions. Children naturally ask deep questions, most likely because they are not afraid to speak the truth. They have a curiosity that gets stripped away somewhat as they grow. Children don't have the defenses that adults have built up in order to survive. They are immediately focused on what's happening around and to them, whereas adults often shy away from being direct, curious, and truthful, and often get distracted by other cares. Spelunking involves childlike curiosity and the discovery of how to get out. A child has this curiosity, and even riskiness, but we often grow out of that. In haiku we see a light in the darkness and follow it. The following haiku represent to me positive, childlike traits and questions:

Blue dragonfly—
what do you
listen to?

Why do we move?
so we can stand
still

Haiku are healing

Haiku are very brief, like our lives. But they are healing. So they are really a way of stepping out of our lives for a moment—to reflect, to use the childlike parts as well as the shadowy or unknown parts.

Near autumns end
walking with my shadow
in the forest

A bear and her cubs
out the window
joy fills the room

Draw a circle . . .
unmake a point

Fall—
my heart redder
with each leaf

Laughing and crying are similar

Laughing and crying come from the same neurological mechanism. For example, if you cry and cry and cry, you will laugh. And if you laugh, laugh, laugh, you will cry. So the archetypes of laughing and crying are connected.

Why do I laugh?
not far off
tears

Sunflower smiles
the day seems better

Peach-red petals open
spilling sunny fragrance

lone blue flower
open to the morning sun-
glorious

Life and death

Is death final or a new beginning? Of course I hope that death leads to something else, and that we continue on. This is why religions are so popular, as they focus on what happens after death. Once in Japan, I was taken with a friend to a Buddhist gathering, to hear a lecture on a talk about life after death, which is a common theme in Buddhism. Surely, as in nature, life follows the end of everything. Life returns. But what form will we live it in?